Reader Praise
for Walks with Sierra

"You must meet Sierra, also known as "Pup".... a wonderful gift for dog lovers everywhere."

"This is a heartfelt, loving ride."

"I have read many, many animal books over the years but not one has touched me as deeply as "Walks With Sierra".... I have shared my book with several friends, including my vets, and as they pass it on they always tell the people to have the tissues ready."

"Cried and smiled reading your book."

"Beautiful, touching, perceptive. I feel I knew Sierra as an old dear friend."

"The story of your time with Sierra touched my heart in ways that only someone who has loved a dog can know."

"You captured your friend with soul and tenderness. Thank you!"

"The photos are as understated and beautiful as your writing."

"A perfect read — 'reflection' might be a better word — for a few hours of solitude."

Walks with Sierra

The Story of an Old Soul

Liz Brooking

November, 2012

For Jim and Indy

May you always know the love of a dog.

[signature]

For anyone who has ever loved a dog.

This is the story of a stray. In his own words, he tells of the time we spent together in what was to be the last year of his life.

All alone, he simply appeared at my door one cold and blustery November day. He had lost his way — abandoned, no doubt. It was my good fortune that no one ever came to claim him.

I named him Sierra for the strength of the mountains, but you can call him Pup, as I did.

Hello

My name is Sierra.

Well, that's actually my new name as of about a month or so ago. The truth is, I can't even tell you what my real name was before I started my new life, and to be honest, it doesn't really matter.

Because my life — and my story — start now.

An Old Soul

People tell me I'm an old soul.

I guess I'm somewhere between 10 and 14 years old, but nobody knows for sure. Mom says I'm "10 years older than God." I think she is dyslexic and correct her. "Dog," I say, but she doesn't understand me, even though I understand most of what she says, so it still comes out the same.

I may be old, but when I dream, I'm only four. In my dreams, my legs are strong and powerful, my bark is clear and commanding, and I can hunt and play for hours.

In my dreams, my brother is still alive.

But when I awaken, I am old again. Old and stiff, with joints that ache as I rise from my bed, and legs that barely support me at times. But I lift myself to my feet with a smile, because I know that with every nap I take, I can relive the best of my childhood. And when I'm awake, I know that I am well loved.

My Pig Sister

This is Wilma.

She's a big part of my life. I know she's a pig, but she's pretty much like a sister to me.

She knows a thing or two about getting what she wants. Stubborn, obstinate, ok I admit it, irritatingly adorable, but I'd protect her with my life.

I used to try to herd her around, but I've stopped wasting my time. She answers to nobody — unless there is food involved.

Oh, did I tell you? She whinnies like a horse.

A Chance Encounter

I met someone today.

It was just an ordinary day otherwise. I was out by the chapel — an old, one room stone building that abuts the creek. I could hear running water, despite the fact that days earlier it was groaning with ice.

I heard barking, but ignored it; the dogs on the farm bark all the time. But this was different. As it got louder I looked up and I saw him.

He was magnificent, bounding across the field and the creek towards me, all the while ignoring desperate calls for him to return. How I admired him. In seconds he was there, standing right in front of me with lustrous, black coat and taught muscles.

And there we were, lost in a circle of nose to tail dancing. He greeted me, "Hello." But no sooner than we started he was gone.

If you know him, would you please tell me his name? And if you know him, tell him that I'd like him to come and play.

A Starry Night

It was a beautiful night.

We were out on our late night walk — the last one before she tucks me into bed and says, "Good night, Pup," and then reassures me, "I'll see you in the morning."

It was crisply cold and quiet outside, save for the hoot owl. A sky no longer obscured by snow clouds, all midnight blue and sparkling with stars. I had my nose to the ground, sniffing to see what and who had tread here before me.

"Have you ever seen a shooting star, Pup?" She asks me things like this, never really expecting a reply. "I saw six of them in Yosemite once. You would have really liked that."

She points into the distance and says, "There's the big dipper, Pup!" I look up to please her, and think it looks just like what she uses to spoon the broth into my supper. I can't wait for breakfast.

The Ritual

It always starts the same way.

I can hear her coming down the stairs. I try to suppress the wag of my tail, just to hear her whispers as she sits beside me to stroke my head. I rest my paw on her thigh. "I love you too, Momma," I say. And the ritual begins.

"Good mornin' precious Pup," she says, as she moves towards the counter to prepare my feast. We sing our song — always the same song — and I perk my ears in anticipation.

When she's made my meal, I give her distance; I like to watch her place the bowl in its stand. She turns to give me a kiss on the forehead, then it's time to eat.

When I am done, I come to tell her. She rises from her chair to inspect the dish. "How'd you do, old Pup?" she says, knowing full well the bowl will be empty. She opens her arms wide with approval and exclaims, "You did so, so good today!"

I wag my tail, cock my head, and display a sheepish grin to acknowledge that I have done something truly exceptional — again.

Early Morn'

It's that time of day again.

The time when most of the world still sleeps and we meet the morning and its moonlit sky, alone. She turns on the porch light and opens the door to let me out. I stop to take in the view, then gently maneuver the steps to the outside.

The wind picks up and I pause, alert for what it will tell me. "Go left, Mom," I say. She always wants to go to the right, passing the kick out shed and the paddocks to the back of the property. We've done that route three days in a row, I think.

I want to go to the chapel; I know he lives just across the way and perhaps we'll meet again.

There's a brief standoff, but I win. She is too tired this morning to challenge me and I have given her that look which says, "I can outlast you."

Walking towards the chapel, I hear her say, "This is my favorite time of day, Pup." The birds have barely begun to stir. The day is filled with promise. And it's just the two of us — alone with our thoughts and each other.

I nod in agreement, "I like this time best too."

Come Spring

There's a place I want to go.

It's just down the drive, around a corner. As we approach it, I begin to trot. But this game has become a habit, and she is already keeping pace, hovering.

"I am not a child," I explain, my face registering utter frustration and disappointment as she puts her hand on my shoulders to slow me and point me in the other direction.

It's not like I can get lost, I think to myself. I know this road; it's the one we take in the car. I know its twists and bends, and its ruts and rumbles.

I know where the fox passes for his nocturnal hunt, that spot where the deer frantically look for a place to exit, and I've all but memorized the knots in the rotted out tree that's home to someone.

Come spring, when I'm well and able, this will be the first place I go. Promise me something: if I get tired or forget my way, you'll bring me home to my mom.

Love Aplenty

Wilma's personality fills a room.

People come to visit her, always bearing gifts — an old lettuce butt, an apple core, a carrot.

She sleeps under a pile of hay; it's several feet high now. The mound rises and falls with her breath. This they find enchanting. She hears them coming and pokes her head out just enough to inspect the offering without compromising her warmth. Clearly, it meets her approval.

She snorts and whinnies, and they stroke the course black hair on her broad shoulders. She turns onto her side, gently lifting her leg in hopes of a tummy rub.

I go in search of the ferrets, trying to mask my jealousy. "What's the matter, Pup?" I hear my mom say as I wander towards the tack room door. "There's love aplenty."

"Plenty of love to share," she persists. I continue to look for the ferrets.

"You know Pup, I love you to the ends of the earth," she says, one hand on Wilma's belly and the other beckoning me to join them. "Don't you know this by now?"

I stop to consider it. Then I remember, the earth is round; it has no ends. I run to Momma.

From Where I Sit

I watch you from my deck sometimes.

From where I sit, I have a perfect view of the creek below. I see that you are different than the others. The mallards, they drift with the current; you wade the creek in utter silence, and I am transfixed.

They are always together; you are a loner.

There's something primordial about you — spectacular, I think. I marvel at your grace. I have memorized your silhouette. And I wonder, why are you alone, grey heron? Is there nobody quite so fantastic as you?

If you would like a friend, feel free to look my way. My Momma says there's love aplenty, and I would like to learn to fly.

Our Car

This is our car.

I try to keep it in my sights so as not to miss an opportunity to go somewhere. I really don't care much where we go, I just don't want to be left behind.

In our car, we listen to the radio. I practice my English and try to catch her eye in the rear view mirror. I see her smile; she knows I'm making progress.

The rhythms of the road rock me to sleep. Occasionally, I stand to see what I'm missing: a bit of woodland, a stretch of pasture, some bright lights in a dark sky. Sometimes I see a horse and rider — right in the middle of the road. I like to watch their nostrils flare as we stop to let them pass.

Last time we took a ride, we went to the vet. Out of the car, I zigged and zagged all the way around the property, leaving messages on every bush I could reach before she said, "Come on, Pup," and led me inside.

At the end of our visit, we said our goodbyes. I got a treat. They gave Momma a geriatric brochure. I tried to tell them as we walked out the door, "She's really not that old."

At least I don't think so.

The Music Stand

There's a place in a California woods called
The Music Stand.

This place holds a special place in Momma's heart. To
come upon it after a long hike is always a delight. We
found a similar place today, some 3,000 miles away. We
pass this spot every day, but never have we noticed the
turtle sculpture tacked to a tree. "Look Pup!" she says
with a joyous smile, as I gingerly make my way across
the ice that coats our drive. "It's a sign," she exclaims,
catching her balance.

"Is it an amulet? An ornament? Maybe it's an
offering, Pup."

"No Momma," I tell her, "It's just a reminder to
slow down."

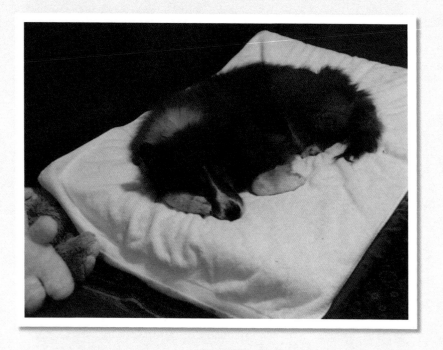

In the Night

She's taken to sleeping on the couch in my room as of late.

In the dark of night, when she hears me stir, she comes to my side. I cough — a weak cough, but a persistent one. One hand on my forehead, the other on my backside, she stills me, comforts me, then cradles my head in her lap and says, "Old age isn't for sissies, my Pup."

Her eyes scan my body like a searchlight. She brushes the dandruff from my once beautiful coat, now a patchwork of ailments. She smoothes the hair on that spot that's just begun to grow in, and she traces an outline of skin where nothing grows anymore.

"Pup, I used to think this was a psychological thing with you. Now, I'm convinced — you've got a metabolic problem."

I tell her it's both.

"We'll get you fixed up," she says and rubs the underbelly of my chin till I am almost lulled to sleep.

We hear a mouse, scratching somewhere behind a wall; he desperately wants to get in — inside where the lights are warm and the comforts real. I think to myself how lucky I am that she invited me to stay.

When, with my eyes, I asked her from her door, "Will you please take care of me?"

"Yes, I will," she said. I will.

Momma, I wonder half asleep, "Did I thank you for being there when I needed you most?"

"Every day, Pup," she says. Every day.

Monochrome World

I watched the white light fill the house from my bed this morning.

Too tired to rise before sunrise. As the sun came through the windowpanes, the objects in my room went to black. The room became a series of meaningless shapes — a backdrop for my thoughts.

"Why so tired?" I pondered as I returned my head to the fleece beneath me. Has the winter caused me to hibernate?

We take our walk before breakfast, moving slowly through a monochrome world.

The drive is icy — scarred and gutted by a plow the night before. Shades of grey and brown amidst colored ice, dirtied from the detritus of that tree and the last melt.

The plow has turned the snow over in piles — manmade drifts which smell of the place from where they came. Confusing. It throws me to smell the barn so far down the road.

Random red berries litter the ground. Not much of a meal, I think, but a splash of color to remind me that someday it will be spring.

Come, spring. Come.

The Otter

Momma saw you first.

I was busy poking my nose under wet snow, thawed just enough to walk on without slipping. "Look, Pup!" she said, distracting me from what I was doing. "There he is."

Just up from the riffle, where the creek makes sounds like so much white noise, you were there. Swimming. Gliding, really. Head above water, you left a small wake — a line like the trail of an airplane in flight.

"It's an otter, Pup."

A beaver, I think. The one who has left his mark on the old sycamore tree.

How brave you are to take to the water like that. It's cold and icy there. When I was a young pup, I could swim. Maybe when the weather is warmer, you'll remind me how.

The Kill

I saw her move to avoid it.

She stepped to the side and steered our walk in a different direction, thinking this would distract me.

Blood-drenched snow — after a day or so, the intensity of its color now fading, like an old bed sheet on a laundry line.

I think it made her shudder, imagining the rabbit the fox had seized under a sliver of moon. Its heart racing, until it all but exploded in a warm embrace. A cry, then stillness. A spasm, then nothing.

I see the pink snow clearly. How lucky, I think. A warm meal. A reward. A hunt well executed. And the snow, now drenched with protein, a gift left behind for someone like me.

A month or so ago I would have been so grateful for the leftovers.

False Spring

Even the birds slept in today.

A blanket of snow an inch or so thick covers the ground.
It's peaceful, I think as I christen the white path in front
of me.

Yesterday was so warm. The ice and snow had melted,
making every drive and gully a conduit for water.
Birds were frolicking on damp ground — drunk on a
false spring.

Come dusk, moisture was in the air. There was a different
kind of sky — chalky grey, like gouache so thick. Not a
star in sight.

I could have predicted it, this snow; just yesterday I saw
my shadow. It was so big.

Shadows

I am obsessed with shadows.

By day or moonlight, the thickets and trees near my
house cast a virtual latticework across my path. A basket.
A loosely knit sweater of vines. A net.

It makes me wonder about the squirrel that brazenly
defies gravity. A vertical climb up a trunk, then a leap
from one branch to another. He seems to know the
circuitous path by heart. Muscle memory, I think.

Like an acrobat he skirts the branches, daring them to
bow from his weight before he finds that stronger limb
— the one that will lead him clear across the creek.

"Stop!" I bark as I run to catch up with him. Be careful, I
want to say; those are just shadows, not a net to catch you
when you fall.

Good Company

Momma says I'm good company.

You know that kind of friend, the one that makes you feel good just to be in their presence. No need for talking (a shortcoming of mine); you just enjoy one another's company. Well, she's that kind of friend to me. And I count myself lucky.

We had a lazy day today. It was a warm day, warm enough to open every door and let the breeze waft through the house.

We moved from the front stoop to the deck — chasing the sun. Soaking it in. Letting it warm our brows. Feeling the heat soothe our backbones. She with a book, I with my thoughts. It was lovely.

The birds were all a chatter, making it hard for me to nap. And the rooster 'cross the creek was still crowing well into the afternoon. A celebration of sorts, but one I chose to acknowledge horizontally.

Lilly

It happened again the other day.

It always takes me by surprise — this pain, then total loss of control. I falter, and as my legs buckle, she is there beside me to brace my fall. I collapse to the ground. Defeated. Bewildered. Distressed.

We were out by the barn just down the drive. We started to climb, by the paddock and up the hill, towards that tree with which she is so taken.

My front leg twitches, in solidarity I think, with the hind legs that are about to fail me. She sees my awkward gait. Her arms wrap 'round me. "It's okay, Pup." she says as I try to collect myself. I need a moment to reorient, to regain the trust in my appendages.

As she comforts me, the young mare approaches us. Slowly she moves. Curious. Concerned. Lilly, I think she's called. To my surprise, Momma consoles her too. "It's okay, sweet thing," she says as she extends her hand to stroke a velvety muzzle. "We'll be fine. This happens sometimes."

The Tree

There's a tree on the hill.

Like a guardian it stands, a sentry and protector. It must have been here for generations, I think. So massive are its branches, so prolific its fruit.

On its limbs, the sun just shimmers. Upon closer inspection, I see what look like gumdrops — crystalline gumdrops. Masses and masses of seedpods, encased in ice.

She sees them too. "Gifts to the future, Pup," she says with a fondness. I try to catch her meaning.

"Another tree to climb," she continues. "A good place to build a nest, or a trunk on which to shed one's antlers."

A place to rest in shade next summer, I think. I love this tree too.

The Ruin

I think about who must've lived here one hundred years ago.

This place has a history; I can smell it in the ruin. I smell the ashes from a fire stoked long ago. The scent of a young girl still clings to a rag doll, discarded the day she went off to marry — now just dust in a corner. I sniff it to see what I can learn.

Must've been the farrier she married, I suppose. No one else had reason to come here so far from the village.

Our tree on the hill was just a seedling when she was alive. I wonder, does she still walk that hill? Or amble down the drive, just to hear the stream rush to meet the creek? Does she accompany us on our walks under the full moon, just another shadow among so many? And will she walk with me still, when I too am long dead and gone?

A Tribute

You think we can't see you, but we always do.

We came upon you this time in a field. Grazing. Ravenous. Indiscriminately taking all. Neither seedling nor sapling will survive.

When you notice us you freeze. The tension so high, even I can hear your hearts racing. In unison you break for the woods, crashing through stream and thicket, white tails high.

I count. There are fewer of you now. Just five; a doe is missing.

Perhaps that explains the sky tonight. Infused with vermilion, as if to acknowledge the fallen doe. An orange vest, a crossbow — so swift. Almost silent death. A cold eye and a blood drenched forest floor.

The sky is so beautiful tonight. A tribute, I think, to you. Then I hear her say, "Score one for the trees, Pup."

On His Watch

"Did this happen on your watch?" I ask the old tree.

He stands in silence, shamed, I think, by his inability to tell me. Yes, he saw it happen.

They have filled every hole in the drive with something foreign. This rock is grey. The wrong grey; it does not belong here. I sniff it to tell its origin. Like a dream, the answer lies just out of my grasp; I cannot place it.

It is dry and dusty, this rock. No earthy rains have soaked it to give it life. No moss. No hint of the lichen that has made a homestead of our rocks here. No marble in its veins. From where did it come, I wonder?

The ruts and rumbles of my favorite drive have been unforgivably altered. And what of the terrible scars left by its absence somewhere else far away?

Nothing is left to collect that thin layer of ice I like to step on, just to hear the crackle beneath me. There are no more puddles to splash through.

"It's okay, Pup," Momma says, sensing my confusion. "Give it a month or two. There'll be just as many potholes. Enough to play."

Room Enough

For a moment, I thought our pair of geese had left us.

So many were there in the misty morning sky — scores of them. In formation. All order and disorder. They'll get there, I think, regardless of weather.

We stop to take in the sight, drinking in their clamorous sounds. From a distance their atonal calls begin to sound in tune, their chorus somehow peaceful.

A pair has taken to roost in the nearby creek, leaving the flock behind. Today we come upon them feeding in the field.

I run to say hello but I am met with an aggressive stance. His wings spread widely, beat frantically. He is far bigger than I imagined. "Stay away," he signals, as if to say, "This is mine, this land."

Yours, I think? It is mine. We walk it every day. I look to Momma to clear my confusion.

"Pup," she says, "There's room enough for all of us." Ok, I decide. I'll share — but be he had better be nice.

The Way Home

Like fossils they are.

Temporary imprints that come and go with the freeze and the thaw. They tell me who was here before the cold turned the muck to a hardened mass. I take comfort in knowing I do not travel this road alone.

By now I know these prints well: that's the hand that tends to the horses, and Wilma, my pig sister. A deer was here before the temperature dropped.

And those are Momma's boots. They show me the way home.

The Mirror

Yesterday I saw myself in a mirror.

There it was. My blue collar — the one link I have to my past, the only thing I brought with me when I found myself here months ago, confused, cold, and so hungry.

It made me wonder. Do they miss me? Did they look for me? Do they know where I am? Sometimes I dream about them, but in my dreams, it is not really them. And those are not their faces. It is but a feeling I have, not reality. It makes me realize that the tenuous link that binds me to them is beginning to slip away.

I capture Momma's smile in that same mirror. There are now two of her and I am reminded of my good fortune.

Momma says my past is important. After all, it made me who I am. But she also tells me to live in the present.

"Aren't we lucky, Pup?" she says. "We found each other."

"Yes, Momma," I tell her. "I am happy this is my present — and you are not just a dream."

The Woodpecker

Rap, tap 'n tap. Rap, tap 'n tap.

There he goes again. It's early, but the woodpecker has come to say good morning.

He is knocking, tapping at the walls of our house, as if there weren't enough old trees to call his own.

Through the window I spot him. His red head is a flash of welcomed color. Beautiful though he is, I must tell him, "This is our time; please don't take away from it.

"Momma has to go to work soon. Once she's gone, we can play for hours."

Restless

The house sounds are different tonight.

Though Momma has been asleep for hours, I sit lost in my thoughts. I cannot sleep. Something is in the air — I can feel it.

I get up and walk to her bedside. I listen for her breath. She is still breathing. I find a piece of exposed skin on which to rest my cold nose. Yes, she is awake!

"Pup," she says. "It's 2 o'clock in the morning. Go to bed."

I circle around a few times to find a better spot by her side. When she withdraws her hand and hides it under the covers, I finally succumb. But those sounds. There is something in the wind. Does she not hear it?

At 3 o'clock, I rise again. Momma, please wake up. She begs me to sleep. "Please, Pup. Get some rest."

I watch the clock, counting the hours till morning. They pass so slowly. It is a long night and I am restless. At 5 o'clock I hear her stir. My tags jingle as I jump to my feet. Hurry Momma, I think, and my tail begins to wag.

This time she rises from the couch to say, "Okay, Pup. Let's go greet the day."

"Quickly, Momma," I say as I bolt through the door.

There is something in the wind. Could it be spring? Please make it spring!

The Scavenger

I am but a scavenger.

A master at finding that one mess of feathers in a far field. I have a nose for it. Blood soaked snow. A random bone with just enough marrow to get me through a cold night.

There is no shame in having stolen the last of the nutrients from another's full belly. Scat and manure, they once sustained me.

Today, behind the fallen tree I found her. A doe. Well, a part of one. Something had dragged this leg far from its body. Still left beside the road, I imagine. A twisted, hardened mass. Turkey vultures picking away at it, daring the cars to disturb their feed.

I picked the leg up to bring it to Momma. There are few gifts I can give her, you know.

"Pup," she says to me. "Look what you found! But that is sustenance for some poor soul, and you have a warm meal waiting at home."

Last Storm

I realize that I am an old man.

I feel it as I brace for the wind this morning. In its arms, a million snowflakes. Traveling horizontally. Catching an updraft. Falling in time to muffle all sounds. Blanketing the world around me.

The snow settles on my brow. I stop to take it all in. I want to feel the cold melt in my eyelashes, for this may be our last storm. This may be my last winter.

A week ago, I saw the bulbs had broken through. A bit of brilliant green fooled by warmer weather, today assaulted by white beauty. Will they survive the cold, as I have this year?

If this should be my last storm, I want to remember all of it: its fury, its majesty, the peace it brings me.

I marvel at its commitment to still us all, if just for this day.

Locomotion

She likes to play this game with me.

And I happily indulge her. She pretends I can run faster; I pretend she can. It's a kind of give and take, with one of us picking up the lead, then falling back just long enough to allow the other a brief win. It makes her laugh.

Usually, I win. After all, I do have twice as many legs.

I may have a hard time just getting up from the floor most of the time, but I've pretty much mastered the art of locomotion.

Yesterday we played our game again. It was a good day.

Inventory

She has given me something to call my own.

Two bones. One made of rawhide, the other, a soup bone just big enough to be a challenge.

With these new possessions the hours pass without notice. So content am I to sit and chew until I fall exhausted and ready for a well-earned nap. A bone by my side. Just within reach. Always in sight.

Sometimes Momma moves it so I have buried the rawhide bone outside where not a soul can find it. And each day before we walk, I inspect my inventory.

"It is still there," I say to myself, relieved. I can now go about my business, until I determine that a newer, safer place is required.

Constant Companion

Momma says that's the same moon.

The one that shone so brightly last night, but only faintly hints of his enormous power in the dusk of this grey evening.

It is the same moon that has lit the sky for generations, she tells me. Acting as a beacon. A comfort in a pitch-black night.

Sometimes, just a trace of his face he'll show us. On another night he will be a most brilliant orb, and I will get no sleep for his brightness.

He is our constant companion, and for this I am glad.

Simple Pleasures

I'm a lucky Pup.

Simple pleasures are mine for the taking. Like a roll in the grass on a day that could well be spring. The snow has finally melted.

With the birds I laugh along, thinking of what's to come.

The Fox

You and I, we are not so different.

I see myself in you. Your luxe red coat. Ears at attention. We were simply separated by evolution. I hear your barking at night and I know we are somehow one in the same.

Isolated by a creek. A frost covered field. The comfort of my elevated deck. Yes, I see that you stare at me. With ears up, you listen for movement — a sign that I might join you. Not today.

Like me, you feel the chill in the air. The grasses — you see them too. That strange geometry of frosted shapes that challenge the claim that it is now spring. The blade that catches the light, flickering like a random sliver of mica in dirt.

You are very still. So confident. Too much so, I think. For I too know that the goslings are there by the water, born last week. I have met their mother, and you will be no match.

Spring Storm

The storm came on so quickly.

Purposefully. A blue sky suddenly turned angry.
The wind picked up with a force. I liked the feel of it —
the excitement.

I squinted through the bright light of a sunset trying to
show itself through thick clouds on the move. The air
filled my nostrils.

A crack. A rumble. Then the storm was upon us. Squid
ink sky. Then pounding rain, as if to demand our
attention. A hail of white pearls bounced from the deck.
Momma and I watched in fascination.

It must be spring. "I wonder, Momma, is it really here?"

"Yes, it's so, Pup. Finally, it is here."

Lone Goose

For days we have watched you.

Circling the farm, searching. Alone. Frantic. Your belly lit
by morning sun, its shape changes with every breath as
you expel what sounds like desperation.

Your calls tell me of your sorrow, your confusion.

Where is your mate, my friend? Did the fox take a meal
at your expense? I have not seen the feathers, but I know
what it feels like to be abandoned, to lose a loved one.

Do not despair. You are not alone, for I hear your calls.
And Momma and I will keep you company.

Too Late

She is too late.

I try to stop myself, but I am lost. Lost in a private battleground. Out of control, but in total command. With every bite, I stifle the itch.

I stop to catch my breath and suddenly the urge is silenced by the sting of air on raw flesh. What is left of my fur is now soaked in saliva. I have done it — again.

I pace and pace, waiting for her return. My bare flank now exposed for what it is: old, atrophied, and hot with inflammation. Like raw meat in a window; Soutine's butcher shop carcass.

Finally, I hear our car in the drive. She calls my name with a smile. "Pup!" she says as she opens the door and stoops to greet me. Then she sees my matted, wet hair.

"Oh, Pup," she sighs this time as her eyes well up with tears. She opens her arms to me and I fall into her embrace. Momma is finally home.

It will be ok, now. Momma is home.

Mornings Like This

It is mornings like this when we see him.

When the mist above the pond is as high as the treetops. The geese have just entered the water after deep slumber, goslings in tow. And dew splashes about our legs as we traipse through the grasses.

The heron lifts himself from his perch, unsure the tree is safe enough. His flight across the pond, above the mist, is magical. Graceful. Quiet. Unlike the others, he does not sound a warning but alights in silence. He is alone. Save for the geese, this is his pond. We are intruders.

I watch with awe and some relief, for I have not yet learned to fly. Now, it seems, I may have another chance.

Our Stream

We share a stream.

Sometimes, when we reach that stretch of water down by the falls, we find her there. A doe standing partly in shadow, dappled light on her shoulders where sunshine has broken through the trees that line our stream bank.

She drinks, as I do, from this very spot. The water, which washes over the rocks with such force, has dulled the announcement of our arrival. Our presence still unknown, I immerse my paws in the water.

Cold. Refreshing. It is alive and all around me. I lean down to take it in and notice that our doe has now leapt to safety. No matter. We will meet again, I am sure.

Underground World

I've found almost all of them, I think.

There's one right here, where the tall grasses part ever so slightly. "Momma," I beckon, as I bury my nose in its scent. "Come. I want to show you."

"A hole, Pup!" she exclaims.

"No, Momma. An entrance to another world," I tell her. "A labyrinth of tunnels lies beneath us, you see, stretching the length of the property and beyond."

By my count, there's one just west of our house, within the stand of trees. Another sits at the base of our 40-foot pine. Where the hill rolls off towards town, I remember three. And there must be many — so many — in the meadow, which seems to go on forever.

As I survey the horizon, I wonder who lives here, in this underground world. Do they move about in total darkness? How, Momma? How can they live without this view?

The Artist

I must learn to do this, I think.

To start each day with such flourish. Surely, I would be tapped of strength before I even started.

How I admire you, old sun. While I spend my days napping, it seems that you take your rest only when the moon steps in to stay you.

You are an artist, my friend. Do not put down your brush; it suits you.

Song of Sorrow

It was 4:39 a.m. — the moment of your passing.

Your cries awakened me from a dream. Silenced by your outrage, even the birds froze at attention, huddling closer, instinctively seeking the comfort of one another.

While you were wriggling desperately to free yourself, I sat immobilized, listening, imagining, shuddering at the thoughts that carried me to where you were — suffering all alone.

Blood pooled in a corner of his mouth. He released his grasp, just long enough for you to let out one last cry. I waited, anticipating. There was no one to come to your rescue. He barked with satisfaction. Again, I heard it. It was almost as if he were laughing; bragging, over a life extinguished.

The minutes passed. A drama now over, the birds began to sing again, led first by the morning dove. A song of sorrow. A song of peace.

Grateful

I wonder still how I managed to find you.

Of all the people in the world, how is it that our paths crossed? Why did you open your door to take me in? Why comfort me and save me from the cold?

I was invisible. Plenty had passed me without notice. Nobody stopped to look into my eyes. A stranger I was, alone in this world. "Why, Momma, when others were blind to me, did you choose to see? Why rescue me?"

"My precious Pup," she says as she kisses my forehead. "Don't you know by now? It was you, Pup; it was you, who rescued me."

I lean towards her whispers and the comfort of her voice and I think.

"Yes, Momma, I guess I knew that. But I am grateful, ever so grateful, anyway."

Fireflies

The day began early; I hope it is a long one.

Up at 3:30, I pace the room, now a makeshift infirmary. Moving from towel to towel, searching for one not yet damp with my own urine.

The windows are open and I am drawn to what is calling me. I hear the peepers — and something else too. Despite the hour, Momma is up now, pulling on her boots. She has understood.

We step into the world outside our house and begin our walk. Through diaphanous mist we tread, slowly, for it is dark. The clouds have all but obscured our moon. A rain of tears will wash the sky this special morning.

We wander up the drive, passing my favorite trees; paper cutouts in a murky wash. Intermittent flickers of light dance around us. Teasing us to come further. Into the meadow. Down the hill. They seem tentative. Unsure. But they do not leave us.

"Look Pup," Momma whispers, for it is still very early and not even the birds have awakened yet. "My precious Pup, do you see the fireflies?" she asks.

"I see Momma, but those are not fireflies. It is a host of angels come to show me the way. Do not be sad. I will tell them to wait, but not too long. Don't be sad. I am not quite ready yet."

The Symphony

I heard their calls again this evening.

Momma accompanied me on a walk in a pitch-black night. Then together we sat in front of the house, in silence, save for the symphony around us. The rhythmic base of the bullfrog. The high-pitched trill of cicadas. The sound of our own breathing.

Under our moon she comforted me while I did my best to tap into the life forces around us, hoping to imbue myself with their energy, if only to steal a few more hours.

"Pup," she said to me. "I love you till the ends of the earth."

I put my head in her lap to tell her it will be ok. The fireflies are out tonight, but they have kept a respectful distance.

Impression

I never noticed it before so it got me to thinking.

Just outside the barn, there's a tiny handprint that marks the spot where one small soul has been. Declaring his presence. Leaving an impression. An indelible reminder. His mark on this world.

Where, I wonder, is this little boy now? I look up at Momma and ask her to wait. We pause for a moment. Have I made such an impression that I will be so remembered?

When you see a sky shot with vermilion, Momma, will it remind you of me? When the fury of a winter storm stills all that it touches, will you think of me then?

If I should have to go someday, when a light rain kisses your face, know that it is just me, Momma. I have come back to say hello.

Shades of Green

"How many shades of green make up this view of mine?"

I ask her this as we wander somewhat aimlessly today.

"As many as there are shades of brown in your lovely coat, I suppose, my Pup," she says as she smiles at me.

"As many, Momma, as there are shades of white in a winter landscape?"

"Yes, Pup. At least that many."

"As many colors as light our sky at sunrise, Momma?"

"I suppose that's so, Pup."

"What about the leaves of fall? Do you think our trees will turn shades of amber?"

"Of that, I am sure, Pup."

"Let's play a game, Momma. I'm thinking of a color…"

Sparkle

I can feel my strength returning.

"There's a sparkle in your eyes again, my Pup," Momma tells me as she places my breakfast in the bowl.

"I know," I tell her with a wag of my tail. "I am feeling better now."

Maybe tomorrow we can go down to the stream by the falls. My friend, the doe, must have wondered where I have been all this time.

Make it Shine

How I long for a sunny day.

It has rained for days now. Seventeen to be exact; I have counted them.

Even the grasses bend in utter defeat. Their own weight, they can no longer bear. The dogwood blossoms have all but given up; most lie on the ground — spent before I could fully enjoy them.

And that beautiful, old tree, it has fallen into the pond. Ground so soaked it could not support it. Uprooted. Taproot snapped, severed from essential lifeblood. Not even the caretaker can help it now.

I have all but memorized the confines of my room. The creases in my bedding are too familiar to me, and I miss the light that once filtered through our house.

Oh, how I wish for the sun to shine. Please Momma, make it shine.

Blue Sky

I knew she could do it.

When she opened the screen door we saw it — blue sky for miles. Even the clouds looked happy to me. They have done their business for days. Now the stream is full, the trees are stripped of tired limbs, and the weak among us have stepped aside. It is time to rest.

"Look, Pup! The rain is gone," says Momma incredulously.

"I know Momma," I reply. "I told you, you could make it so.

"But why, if you can make the sun shine, can't you make me something else for breakfast?"

Our Field

I miss our field, Momma.

What took all of spring to grow was laid bare in the course of last evening, before the first of summer. The hum of heavy equipment. Tractors so large, they covered much ground.

Grasses, once meters high, systematically fell, exposing the contours of the earth, and a myriad of holes leading somewhere. It is man over nature.

The clover, the wildflowers, none stood a chance. What once gracefully bowed to the wind is now a series of short dry stalks. Felled by metal blades, they share no resemblance to their former selves.

Slashed and bailed, they will sit in the sun only to be hauled someplace far away. It is uncomfortable under foot. I carefully choose my path, following the trail left by tire tracks.

The ruts and furrows remind me that our deer now have one less place to hide.

A Meal to Remember

I watched her from my rug in the kitchen, as I always do.

First she cut the lamb. An entire leg she carved, just out of reach on the countertop. Juices ran onto a cutting board. She did not discard the fat.

Great hunks of meat she then placed on our grill. Would she eat this without me? For a moment, I actually wondered. In minutes, the sizzle and smell were almost enough to sate me. But there she did not stop.

Carrots in water came to a rolling boil. She tested them. Are they done, Momma? Not too hot, please. And rice. Not just any rice — brown rice for me.

Today she made me a meal to remember. All of this she laid before me. I watched her place my bowl on the floor. As she bent down she kissed my forehead. "I love you Pup," she told me, as she always does.

I know, Momma. To the ends of the earth, I love you too.

Too Early

The bushes are everywhere.

Throughout the property, I have seen them as we take our walks. It seems they were all just in flower.

She eyes the bright red berries, glistening in sunshine. Not yet ripe — but begging to be picked. "Too early," Momma says with a sigh. We must watch them, she explains.

"The birds will know they've ripened long before we do, Pup."

I study her face. The birds? Must we fight for our fair share? I am now concerned.

"When it gets closer, I will stand look out. But Momma," I tell her. "You must hold the basket."

Burl Wood

I know somebody's in there.

While all else is faltering, my nose has yet to fail me. Today it has brought me here, to this old tree.

The tree with the big knot of burl wood, just large enough to hide its hole. Bulbuous. Irregular. Curiously golden in contrast to the grey bark from which it has emerged. It is too big for me to climb.

I point for Momma. I sniff again. "Do not be afraid," I try to tell him with a wag of my tail. "I just want to ask you to come out and play."

Unfinished Business

Not yet, I plead.

Don't rush me, Momma. This, I try to impress upon her, is important.

"Come on, sweet Pup," she calls me. There's a scent on the bark of our beech tree and I am trying to decipher it. I ignore her second request.

She comes closer to cajole me. Now I am determined. Stubborn. Slightly annoyed. I have unfinished business to attend.

I back out from under the branches. I look her in the eye. "Momma, why must you hurry me?"

Missing You

I think about you from my hospital room.

It is strange to sleep here without you nearby. Without the comfort of your breathing. Amid the whimpers of a stranger next door.

I have had a full life. And I am tired. I rest my head, grateful for the soft quilt beneath me. It still smells of you, Momma. My mind wanders and I imagine that you are still here by my side. I feel the warmth of your body. The safety of your presence.

You were curiously quiet today. I saw you hide your tears to give me strength. It's ok to cry. Today was our last walk to the waterfall, wasn't it? It has been ages since I had the strength. Funny, how the day progressed.

As I give in to slumber, I imagine your kiss on my forehead. I hear the tenderness of your voice. "I love you till the ends of the earth," you say in my dream. I can see you in my gaze, Momma. My greying muzzle rests happily in your hand, and all the world knows just how much it is that you love me.

You are part of me now. How lucky I was to have found you, to have loved you, and to be so loved.

When the rain kisses your face, Momma, remember, it will be me. Just me — missing you.

Homecoming

Today was my homecoming.

My joy was tempered by utter exhaustion and the look on Momma's face when the doctors gave her the word. I know her tears well.

I am an old man, Momma. This we knew from the start. So, let us make the most of each day I am granted. "Try to live in the present," I can still hear her say. I must remind her of this.

The indignities of life, they are not unique to me. Yet it still surprised me when the geese did not scurry to safety at the mere site of me today.

A lone bird has signaled all of my arrival and I am now greeted by song. It shall help me to sleep today. Yes, I think I will sleep well; I am home.

Want for Nothing

In my dreams, I'm a young pup again.

Eager to hunt and play, I rise without effort. My eyes do not deceive me, and my steps are steady and sure. All steel and stealth am I.

In my dreams, my formidable presence sends the birds to flight. Even my shadow makes the geese scurry. Squirrels scramble for the safety of the trees and I revel at the site of it all. But it is just play to me; I mean them no harm.

I am alive in every fiber of my being. And I want for nothing.

Everlasting

We have come full circle, you and I.

Today you made me scrambled eggs. That was our first meal together, Momma. Do you remember? That day I came to your door and asked you with my eyes, "Would you take me in?" You said yes.

"Yes, sweet Pup. I will take care of you."

Then I ate my eggs ravenously. With as much gusto as a tired soul could muster. I was grateful. I was nervous. I had never known such kindness.

Today, I ate eggs from your hand. One mouthful at a time. Tentatively, as I wrestled with a question. Am I confusing my love for you with hunger?

Momma, I have no appetite. This I have tried to tell you. But you are there, with food in hand. So I eat to comfort you now.

Be merciful, Momma. I am an old soul and it is as you have said, "I can not keep you for myself, my Pup." There are others, many others, who are calling me.

I wonder, "Like our friend the moon, will I too live on for generations?"

"Yes, my Pup," you assure me as you stroke my forehead. "You have left an indelible mark on this world. You have touched my heart. You, my blessed, are everlasting."

Certain Things We Know

There are certain things we know; we intuit.

Death has hounded me for months. I can even smell it
on my breath. We've done a masterful job of staying just
ahead of it, outrunning it, outsmarting it. But it is the
natural order of things, Momma, and death is relentless.

I see it every day in our walks: a carcass stripped clean,
the shell of a Robin's egg. I hear the cries at the climax of
a hunt. They are all just outside our window, beyond the
comfort of our door.

"Look, Pup!" you said to me last night as we took our
walk near the pond. "It looks like heat lightening."

"But Momma, we both know," I replied with a look. "It is
the fireflies again, and this time I am ready.

"It is time now for you to let me go."

We Shall Meet Again

Not yet 24 hours have passed since I left you.

Already though, much has happened and I feel a burden lifted. I have been back to the ruin, Momma, and she was there. It was as though she expected me. She rose from the stoop with doll in hand and a warm smile to greet me.

"You have come to keep me company, Pup!" she exclaimed. "I am so happy to see you."

Then she motioned for me to follow. We wandered down the drive, where you and I first met, and where we once felt her presence. Where the stream still rushes to the meet the creek. Then up the hill she led me to our tree, the one of which you were so fond.

Oh Momma, how I'll miss your company. But I am comforted to know, as I watch you sleeping fitfully now, that when you wake, you will feel my presence. You will know that I have come to visit.

It was not by chance that I found you, Momma. We were destined to be together, and we shall meet again.

I must leave you for now, as she is calling me. "Come sweet Pup," she beckons. "We must go. It is time to tell the heron that you have finally learned how to fly."

Yes, Momma, I can fly. It is wonderful. I am graceful. And I am free.

With Me Always

This they have never done before.

The geese were all just outside our house this morning, Pup. It was curious. I walked the drive to meet them and they did not rush off. Instead they watched me, unafraid.

One in particular did not take his eyes from me. The others calmly stretched. They ate in silence, slowly picking at the grasses in the morning sun.

They have come to acknowledge your death, I thought to myself. They miss you as I do. No longer do you trot down their hill in chase, just to see the beauty of their flight.

It was peaceful. A display of solidarity and compassion. For minutes we said nothing. Then, I greeted them. "I know, he is gone," I said. "And I miss him too."

At this they began to turn away. Towards the pond they ambled, one-by-one, he being the last to rise. It was then that I saw it. The goose, whose eyes would not leave me, turned towards the water and began to walk. His gait was uneven. Just a slight limp. A lack of control. That's when I knew. It was you, sweet Pup.

Thank you, my Pup, for everything. I love you to the ends of the earth, and you will be with me always.

Sierra,
Your visit was far too brief, but we had a good run
and for that I am grateful.

Made in the USA
Charleston, SC
09 November 2012